Name: _____ Class: _____

Table of Contents

Introduction	2
NY-3.OA.3	3
Use multiplication and division within 100 to solve word problems in situations involving equal groups, arrays, and measurement quantities.	
NY-3.OA.8	18
Solve two-step word problems posed with whole numbers and having whole-number answers using the four operations.	
NY-3.NF.1	33
Understand a unit fraction, 1/b, is the quantity formed by 1 part when a whole is partitioned into b equal parts. Understand a fraction a/b as the quantity formed by a parts of size 1/b.	
Proficiency Check 1	50
Proficiency Check 2	66
About Us	82

Introduction

This workbook was created to help your students ace the math state exams. It covers the most important standards that are commonly found on the New York state math tests from 2012-2019. Each standard has at least two guided problems and several practice problems that can be done together or individually. The guided problems can be accessed by scanning the QR code or entering the short link into your browser.

These problems are designed to help your students show improvement and mastery over the high-priority standards when they take the math state exam.

Grade 3 Topics:

1. Operations and Algebraic Thinking
    a. Represent and solve problems involving multiplication and division.
    b. Solve problems involving the four operations, and identify and extend patterns in arithmetic.
2. Number and Operations – Fractions
    a. Develop understanding of fractions as numbers.

Note: Fractions are limited to those with denominators 2, 3, 4, 6, and 8.

Grade 3 High Priority New York State Math Standards:

1. NY-3.OA.3 Use multiplication and division within 100 to solve word problems in situations involving equal groups, arrays, and measurement quantities.

2. NY-3.OA.8 Solve two-step word problems posed with whole numbers and having whole-number answers using the four operations.

3. NY-3.NF.1 Understand a unit fraction, $1/b$, is the quantity formed by 1 part when a whole is partitioned into b equal parts. Understand a fraction a/b as the quantity formed by a parts of size $1/b$.

NY-3.OA.3 Use multiplication and division within 100 to solve word problems in situations involving equal groups, arrays, and measurement quantities.

Watch: How many seats will be used for Ms. Roque's 3rd grade outdoor lunch?

(Use multiplication and division within 100 to solve word problems in situations involving equal groups, arrays, and measurement quantities.)

Link: https://rb.gy/lymj97

NY-3.OA.3 Use multiplication and division within 100 to solve word problems in situations involving equal groups, arrays, and measurement quantities.

Independent practice question:

At the checkout counter, there are 6 rows of snacks with 7 different snacks in each row. How many different snack options are there at the checkout counter?

Answer:

There are 42 different snack options at the checkout counter.

At the checkout counter, there are 6 rows of snacks with 7 different snacks in each row. The total number of different snack options is 6 * 7 = 42

6 rows of snacks * 7 different snacks in each row = 42 different snack options.

NY-3.OA.3 Use multiplication and division within 100 to solve word problems in situations involving equal groups, arrays, and measurement quantities.

Independent practice question:

In the other 3rd grade classroom, there are 3 rows of chairs, with 8 chairs in each row. How many chairs are in the classroom?

Answer:

*3 rows of chairs with 8 chairs in each row is 3*8 = 24 chairs in the classroom.*

*3 rows of chairs with 8 chairs in each row is 3*8 = 24 chairs in the classroom.*

*3 rows of chairs * 8 chairs in each row = 24 chairs in the classroom.*

NY-3.OA.3 Use multiplication and division within 100 to solve word problems in situations involving equal groups, arrays, and measurement quantities.

Watch: Determine how many flowers Mr. Yu's 3rd grade class planted.

(Use multiplication and division within 100 to solve word problems in situations involving equal groups, arrays, and measurement quantities.)

Link: https://rb.gy/fqhsnr

NY-3.OA.3 Use multiplication and division within 100 to solve word problems in situations involving equal groups, arrays, and measurement quantities.

Independent practice question:

In Phys. Ed class, the students are put into rows in the gym. If there are 5 rows with 6 students in each row, how many students are in the Phys. Ed class?

Answer:

30 students

5 rows with 6 students in each row, the total number of students in the Phys. Ed class is 5*6 = 30.

5 rows of students * 6 students in each row = 30 students in the Phys. Ed class.

NY-3.OA.3 Use multiplication and division within 100 to solve word problems in situations involving equal groups, arrays, and measurement quantities.

Independent practice question:

At the store, Mr. Yu purchases a package of eggs that have 4 rows with 12 eggs in each row, how many eggs did Mr. Yu purchase at the store?

Answer:

48 eggs.

At the store, Mr. Yu purchases a package of eggs that have 4 rows with 12 eggs in each row, the total number of eggs Mr. Yu purchased is 4*12 = 48.

4 rows of eggs * 12 eggs in each row = 48 eggs.

NY-3.OA.3 Use multiplication and division within 100 to solve word problems in situations involving equal groups, arrays, and measurement quantities.

Watch: Determine how many snowballs each friend will get for the snowball fight.

(Use multiplication and division within 100 to solve word problems in situations involving equal groups, arrays, and measurement quantities.)

Link: https://rb.gy/lsmigp

NY-3.OA.3 Use multiplication and division within 100 to solve word problems in situations involving equal groups, arrays, and measurement quantities.

Independent practice question:

You have Pokémon cards that you arrange into 8 rows with 7 cards in each row. You decide to share the total amount of your cards with 3 of your friends. How many cards do you and each of your friends get?

Answer:

56 Pokémon cards

You have 8 rows with 7 cards in each row. The total amount of your cards is 8*7 = 56 cards You decide to share the total amount of your cards with 3 of your friends, so each of you and your friends will get 56/4 = 14 cards each.

You decide to share the total amount of your cards with 3 of your friends, so each of you and your friends will get 56/4 = 14 cards each.

8 rows of cards * 7 cards in each row = 56 cards
56 cards / 4 friends = 14 cards per person.

NY-3.OA.3 Use multiplication and division within 100 to solve word problems in situations involving equal groups, arrays, and measurement quantities.

Independent practice question:

For a fundraiser, you bake cupcakes. You have 2 trays that have 24 mini cupcakes, and 3 trays of that have 12 cupcakes. What is the total amount of cupcakes that you bake?

Answer:

84 Cupcakes

For the fundraiser, you bake 2 trays of mini cupcakes with 24 cupcakes each, so that's 224 = 48 mini cupcakes.
You also bake 3 trays of cupcakes with 12 cupcakes each, so that's 312 = 36 cupcakes.
The total amount of cupcakes you bake is 48 mini cupcakes + 36 cupcakes = 84 cupcakes.

*2 trays of mini cupcakes * 24 mini cupcakes per tray = 48 mini cupcakes*

*3 trays of cupcakes * 12 cupcakes per tray = 36 cupcakes*
48 mini cupcakes + 36 cupcakes = 84 cupcakes

NY-3.OA.3 Use multiplication and division within 100 to solve word problems in situations involving equal groups, arrays, and measurement quantities.

Watch: Determine how many basketball teams there will be in gym class.

(Use multiplication and division within 100 to solve word problems in situations involving equal groups, arrays, and measurement quantities.)

Link: https://rb.gy/twoavj

NY-3.OA.3 Use multiplication and division within 100 to solve word problems in situations involving equal groups, arrays, and measurement quantities.

Independent practice question:

During a Physical Education class, the students are playing kickball. There are 36 students in the class, and there are 4 teams needed. How many students will be on each team?

Answer:

9 students per team

During a Physical Education class, there are 36 students in the class and 4 teams needed. The number of students in each team is 36/4 = 9 students per team.

36 students / 4 teams = 9 students per team.

NY-3.OA.3 Use multiplication and division within 100 to solve word problems in situations involving equal groups, arrays, and measurement quantities.

Independent practice question:

Your grandmother brings home 1 dozen mini cupcakes. How many cupcakes do you and your 3 siblings each get?

Answer:

3 Mini cupcakes per person

Your grandmother brings home 1 dozen mini cupcakes, which is equal to 12 mini cupcakes.
You and your 3 siblings each get 12 mini cupcakes / 4 siblings = 3 mini cupcakes each.

1 dozen mini cupcakes = 12 mini cupcakes
12 mini cupcakes / 4 siblings = 3 mini cupcakes per person.

NY-3.OA.3 Use multiplication and division within 100 to solve word problems in situations involving equal groups, arrays, and measurement quantities.

Watch: Discover how many books will be given to each group.

(Use multiplication and division within 100 to solve word problems in situations involving equal groups, arrays, and measurement quantities.)

Link: https://rb.gy/u0cuxo

NY-3.OA.3 Use multiplication and division within 100 to solve word problems in situations involving equal groups, arrays, and measurement quantities.

Independent practice question:

Students at P.S.1234 are going on a field trip. There are 75 seats available for a live dance performance. There are 3 classes going on the trip. What is the maximum number of students per class able to attend the trip?

Answer:

25 students per class

There are 75 seats available for the live dance performance and 3 classes going on the trip. Therefore, the maximum number of students per class able to attend the trip is 75 seats / 3 classes = 25 students per class.

75 seats available / 3 classes = 25 students per class.

NY-3.OA.3 Use multiplication and division within 100 to solve word problems in situations involving equal groups, arrays, and measurement quantities.

Independent practice question:

Samantha baked three dozen cookies for a fundraiser and needed to place the cookies into 6 boxes. How many cookies did she place into each box?

Answer:

6 cookies per box

Samantha baked three dozen cookies which is equal to 312=36 cookies.

She needs to place the cookies into 6 boxes, therefore each box will have 36 cookies / 6 boxes = 6 cookies per box.

3 dozen cookies = 312 = 36 cookies
36 cookies / 6 boxes = 6 cookies per box.

NY-3.OA.8 Solve two-step word problems posed with whole numbers and having whole-number answers using the four operations.

Watch: Find out how much money is left for food on the field trip.

(Solve problems involving the four operations, and identify and extend patterns in arithmetic.)

Link: https://rb.gy/izb06m

NY-3.OA.8 Solve two-step word problems posed with whole numbers and having whole-number answers using the four operations.

Independent practice question:

You buy 3 bags of chips that are $2 each. If you have $10, how much money do you have left?

Answer:

$4

*You buy 3 bags of chips that are $2 each, so the total cost for the chips is 3*$2 = $6.*

If you have $10, the money you have left is $10 - $6 = $4.
*3 bags of chips * $2/bag = $6*
$10 - $6 = $4

NY-3.OA.8 Solve two-step word problems posed with whole numbers and having whole-number answers using the four operations.

Independent practice question:

On a bowling trip with 8 students, each ticket cost $7. If $75 was collected for the trip, how much money is remaining for snacks?

Answer:

$19

On a bowling trip with 8 students, the total cost for the tickets is 8 * $7 = $56.

Since $75 was collected for the trip, the money remaining for snacks is $75 - $56 = $19.

8 students * $7/student = $56
$75 - $56 = $19

NY-3.OA.8 Solve two-step word problems posed with whole numbers and having whole-number answers using the four operations.

Watch: Determine how many total points Sanah earned on Class Dojo this week.

(Solve problems involving the four operations, and identify and extend patterns in arithmetic.)

Link: https://rb.gy/zoeir2

NY-3.OA.8 Solve two-step word problems posed with whole numbers and having whole-number answers using the four operations.

Independent practice question:

You need some school supplies for a project. You purchase 2 poster boards for $3 each, and 3 different types of markers and crayons each costing $4 each. What is the total amount of money you spend on supplies?

Answer:

The total amount of money you spend on supplies is $18

*You purchase 2 poster boards for $3 each, so the total cost of poster boards is 2*$3 = $6*

*You purchase 3 different types of markers and crayons each costing $4 each, so the total cost of the markers and crayons is 3*$4 = $12*

The total amount of money you spend on supplies is $6 + $12 = $18

*2 poster board * $3/poster board = $6*
*3 markers/crayons * $4/markers-crayons = $12*
$6 + $12 = $18

NY-3.OA.8 Solve two-step word problems posed with whole numbers and having whole-number answers using the four operations.

Independent practice question:

You and 2 friends go to the deli for lunch where you each purchase a bag of chips for $2 and an apple for $1 each. You also each purchase a breakfast sandwich for $5 each. What is the total amount spent at the deli?

Answer:

The total amount spent at the deli is $24

*You and 2 friends go to the deli for lunch where you each purchase a bag of chips for $2, so the cost for chips is $2*3 = $6*
*An apple is purchased for $1 each, so the cost for apples is $1*3 = $3*

*You also each purchase a breakfast sandwich for $5 each, so the cost for breakfast sandwiches is $5*3 = $15*
The total amount spent at the deli is $6 + $3 + $15 = $24

$2/bag of chips * 3 people = $6
$1/apple * 3 people = $3
$5/breakfast sandwich * 3 people = $15
$6 + $3 + $15 = $24

NY-3.OA.8 Solve two-step word problems posed with whole numbers and having whole-number answers using the four operations.

Watch: Determine how many packages of books Ms. Young still needs to order.

(Solve problems involving the four operations, and identify and extend patterns in arithmetic.)

Link: https://rb.gy/zqayqc

NY-3.OA.8 Solve two-step word problems posed with whole numbers and having whole-number answers using the four operations.

Independent practice question:

If each package of books costs $24 and there are 6 books in each package. *How much does each book cost?*

Answer:

$4 per book

Each package of books costs $24 and there are 6 books in each package. To find out how much each book cost, you need to divide the total cost of the package by the number of books in it. So, $24/6 = $4 per book.

$24/6 = $4 per book.

NY-3.OA.8 Solve two-step word problems posed with whole numbers and having whole-number answers using the four operations.

Independent practice question:

The other third grade class is also in need of books. They have only 2 books, and have a total of 28 students in the class. How many packs of books will they need to purchase if each pack has 6 books?

Answer:

5 packs of books

The other third grade class has a total of 28 students and only 2 books. To purchase enough books for each student, they will need 28 students - 2 books = 26 more books.

If each pack of books has 6 books, then to purchase enough books for each student, they will need to purchase 26 books / 6 books per pack = 4.33 packs of books.

28 students - 2 books = 26 more books
26 books / 6 books per pack = 4.33 packs of books (approximation)

Note: Since books come in packs, they need to purchase at least 5 packs of books because 4.33 packs can't be purchased.

NY-3.OA.8 Solve two-step word problems posed with whole numbers and having whole-number answers using the four operations.

Watch: Determine how many points Team 6 scored in Kahoot.

(Solve problems involving the four operations, and identify and extend patterns in arithmetic.)

Link: https://rb.gy/g7c4l3

NY-3.OA.8 Solve two-step word problems posed with whole numbers and having whole-number answers using the four operations.

Independent practice question:

You get points for helping around the house. Once you reach 50 points, you earn $5. How many more points do you need to reach 100 points?

Points		
Day	Points	
1	16	
2	17	
3	5	
4	27	
5	10	
6	?	
	100	Total

*Use the next blank page for work space.

(answer and explanation on page 31)

Answer:
25 more points

You get points for helping around the house. Once you reach 50 points, you earn $5.
The total points you have earned so far are 16+17+5+27+10 = 75 points
To reach 100 points, you need to earn 100 points - 75 points = 25 more points.

16+17+5+27+10 = 75 points
100-75 = 25 points

NY-3.OA.8 Solve two-step word problems posed with whole numbers and having whole-number answers using the four operations.

Watch: Determine how much money is left over after purchasing food items from the grocery store.

(Solve problems involving the four operations, and identify and extend patterns in arithmetic.)

Link: https://rb.gy/ljn9ex

NY-3.OA.8 Solve two-step word problems posed with whole numbers and having whole-number answers using the four operations.

Independent practice question:

You go to your school fair with a total of $12. You buy a hamburger for $3, water for $1 and tickets for rides for $6. How much money do you have remaining for games?

Answer:

$2

You go to your school fair with a total of $12. You buy a hamburger for $3, water for $1, and tickets for rides for $6.

The total amount spent on hamburger, water, and ride tickets is $3+$1+$6 = $10
Therefore, you have the remaining for games $12-$10 = $2.

$3 + $1 + $6 = $10
$12 - $10 = $2

NY-3.OA.8 Solve two-step word problems posed with whole numbers and having whole-number answers using the four operations.

Independent practice question:

You help your grandmother by going grocery shopping for her. She needs milk for $4, bread for $3, eggs for $4, peanut butter for $3 and jelly for $2. She gives you $20 for the groceries and tells you that you can keep the change. How much money do you get to keep?

Answer:

You get to keep $4

The total cost of the groceries is $4 + $3 + $4 + $3 + $2 = $16
She gives you $20 for the groceries and tells you that you can keep the change, so the amount you get to keep is $20 - $16 = $4.

$4 + $3 + $4 + $3 + $2 = $16
$20 - $16 = $4

NY-3.NF.1 Understand a unit fraction, 1/*b*, is the quantity formed by 1 part when a whole is partitioned into b equal parts. Understand a fraction *a/b* as the quantity formed by a parts of size 1/*b*.

Watch: Determine what fraction of a brownie pan was left for Ms. Quintanilla.

(Develop understanding of fractions as numbers.)

Link: https://rb.gy/yrn3qk

NY-3.NF.1 Understand a unit fraction, 1/*b*, is the quantity formed by 1 part when a whole is partitioned into b equal parts. Understand a fraction *a/b* as the quantity formed by a parts of size 1/*b* .

Independent practice question:

At a pizza party, there were 2 slices of pizza remaining out of the original 8 slices. Write the amount of slices remaining as a fraction. Draw a picture to justify your answer.

Answer:

2/8

At a pizza party, there were 2 slices of pizza remaining out of the original 8 slices.

The fraction of slices remaining can be written as 2/8.

A visual representation of this fraction can be represented by a pizza with 8 slices, and 2 of the slices are remaining.

NY-3.NF.1 Understand a unit fraction, 1/*b*, is the quantity formed by 1 part when a whole is partitioned into b equal parts. Understand a fraction *a/b* as the quantity formed by a parts of size 1/*b* .

Independent practice question:

If there were 2 slices out of the original 8 slices of pizza not eaten, what fraction of the pizza was eaten? How do you know?

Answer:
¾

We know this is true because we are subtracting the fraction of not eaten slices from 1, which represents the whole pizza, and we get a fraction that shows us how much was eaten.

If there were 2 slices out of the original 8 slices of pizza not eaten, the fraction of the pizza that was eaten can be found by subtracting the fraction of not eaten slices from 1.
The fraction of not eaten slices is 2/8

Therefore, the fraction of the pizza that was eaten can be found by subtracting 2/8 from 1, which gives:
1 - 2/8 = 6/8

We know that 6/8 can be simplified as 3/4, so the fraction of pizza that was eaten is 3/4.

We know this is true because we are subtracting the fraction of not eaten slices from 1, which represents the whole pizza, and we get a fraction that shows us how much was eaten.

1 - 2/8 = 6/8 = 3/4

NY-3.NF.1 Understand a unit fraction, $1/b$, is the quantity formed by 1 part when a whole is partitioned into b equal parts. Understand a fraction a/b as the quantity formed by a parts of size $1/b$.

Watch: Determine what fraction of the Peruvian flag is red.

(Develop understanding of fractions as numbers.)

Link: https://t.ly/_nJg

NY-3.NF.1 Understand a unit fraction, 1/*b*, is the quantity formed by 1 part when a whole is partitioned into b equal parts. Understand a fraction *a/b* as the quantity formed by a parts of size 1/*b* .

Independent practice question:

Javier bakes a rectangular cake for his twin sisters. Javier likes funfetti icing, one of his sisters likes chocolate icing, and his other sister likes vanilla icing. He ices the cake equally so that each of the 3 flavors will have the same amount. Draw a picture to determine how much of the cake is iced with vanilla icing.

Answer:

1/3 of the cake is iced with vanilla icing. This can be determined by the visual representation of the rectangular cake divided into 3 equal parts, one part iced with funfetti, one part iced with chocolate, and one part iced with vanilla.

Javier bakes a rectangular cake and ices it equally with 3 different types of icing: funfetti, chocolate and vanilla. Since the cake is iced equally, each flavor of icing will have 1/3 of the cake.

A visual representation of this can be represented by drawing a rectangular cake divided into 3 equal parts, one part iced with funfetti, one part iced with chocolate, and one part iced with vanilla.

Here is a picture of the representation:

| vanilla |

| chocolate |

| funfetti |

Where each "-" represents a side of the rectangular cake, and the "|"s are the icing on the cake, vanilla is on the top, chocolate in the middle and funfetti is on the bottom.
In this way, we can see that 1/3 of the cake is iced with vanilla icing.

NY-3.NF.1 Understand a unit fraction, 1/*b*, is the quantity formed by 1 part when a whole is partitioned into b equal parts. Understand a fraction *a/b* as the quantity formed by a parts of size 1/*b* .

Independent practice question:

Javier's family comes over to celebrate his sisters' birthday and they eat 2/3 of the cake. What fraction of the cake is remaining?

Answer:

⅓

To find the fraction of the cake remaining after 2/3 of the cake has been eaten, we need to subtract 2/3 from 1.

1 - 2/3 = 1 - (2/3) = (3 - 2)/3 = 1/3
So the fraction of the cake that is remaining is 1/3.

NY-3.NF.1 Understand a unit fraction, 1/*b*, is the quantity formed by 1 part when a whole is partitioned into b equal parts. Understand a fraction *a/b* as the quantity formed by a parts of size 1/*b* .

Watch: Determine what part of Mr. Sanchez's 3rd graders' sign must have text.

(Develop understanding of fractions as numbers.)

Link:https://rb.gy/qkrv7l

NY-3.NF.1 Understand a unit fraction, 1/b, is the quantity formed by 1 part when a whole is partitioned into b equal parts. Understand a fraction *a/b* as the quantity formed by a parts of size 1/b.

Independent practice question:

You are creating a birthday sign for your friend. You divide the rectangular paper into 10 equal parts. You want to create a pattern where exactly 5 parts will be colored in blue. What is the fractional amount that represents the blue parts of the paper?

Answer:

The fractional amount that represents the blue parts of the paper is 1/2.

You are dividing the rectangular paper into 10 equal parts and you want to color exactly 5 parts of the paper in blue. To express this as a fraction, we use the number of blue parts as the numerator and the total number of parts as the denominator. So the fraction that represents the blue parts of the paper is 5/10.

However, since 5/10 can be simplified by dividing both the numerator and denominator by 5, we get 1/2 as the simplified fraction.

5/10 = (5/5)/(10/5) = 1/2
So the fractional amount that represents the blue parts of the paper is 1/2.

NY-3.NF.1 Understand a unit fraction, 1/b, is the quantity formed

by 1 part when a whole is partitioned into b equal parts. Understand a fraction *a/b* as the quantity formed by a parts of size 1/b .

Independent practice question::

On the same sign, 2 of the pieces will be colored in green, and the rest will be left uncolored. What is the fractional amount that represents the uncolored parts of the paper?

Answer:

The fractional amount that represents the uncolored parts of the paper is 1/3.

The fractional amount that represents the uncolored parts of the paper can be found by subtracting the fractional amounts of the colored parts from 1.

Since you divided the rectangular paper into 10 equal parts, and 5 parts are colored in blue and 2 parts are colored in green, the uncolored parts are 10-5-2 = 3 parts.
So the fractional amount that represents the uncolored parts of the paper is 3/10.

However, since 3/10 can be simplified by dividing both the numerator and denominator by 3, we get 1/3 as the simplified fraction.

3/10 = (3/3)/(10/3) = ⅓

So the fractional amount that represents the uncolored parts of the paper is 1/3.

NY-3.NF.1 Understand a unit fraction, $1/b$, is the quantity formed by 1 part when a whole is partitioned into b equal parts. Understand a fraction a/b as the quantity formed by a parts of size $1/b$.

Watch: Investigate how much money a community will receive after winning a raffle.

(Develop understanding of fractions as numbers.)

Link: https://rb.gy/xtqyii

NY-3.NF.1 Understand a unit fraction, 1/*b*, is the quantity formed by 1 part when a whole is partitioned into b equal parts. Understand a fraction *a/b* as the quantity formed by a parts of size 1/*b* .

Independent practice question:

At the school carnival, you played 15 games and won 8 prize tickets at each game.
    A. How many prize tickets did you win in all of the games?
    B. If you need 130 prize tickets for a prize, how many more prize tickets do you need to earn?

Answer:

A. To find out how many prize tickets you won in all of the games, you can multiply the number of prize tickets won per game (8) by the number of games played (15).

*8 prize tickets/game * 15 games = 120 prize tickets*

So, you won 120 prize tickets in total.

B. You have already won 120 prize tickets and you need 130 prize tickets for a prize. So you need 130 - 120 = 10 more prize tickets to earn.

NY-3.NF.1 Understand a unit fraction, $1/b$, is the quantity formed by 1 part when a whole is partitioned into b equal parts. Understand a fraction *a/b* as the quantity formed by a parts of size $1/b$.

Independent practice question:

There were 415 books sold at a school book fair that were each $4. What was the total amount of money earned from the school book fair?

Answer:

To find out the total amount of money earned from the school book fair, you need to multiply the number of books sold by the price of each book.

*415 books * $4/book = $1660*

So, the total amount of money earned from the school book fair is $1660

NY-3.NF.1 Understand a unit fraction, $1/b$, is the quantity formed by 1 part when a whole is partitioned into b equal parts. Understand a fraction a/b as the quantity formed by a parts of size $1/b$.

Watch: Use fractions on a number line to determine how many people are eligible to vote.

(Develop understanding of fractions as numbers.)

Link: https://rb.gy/mwwmtf

NY-3.NF.1 Understand a unit fraction, 1/b, is the quantity formed by 1 part when a whole is partitioned into b equal parts. Understand a fraction *a/b* as the quantity formed by a parts of size 1/b.

Independent practice question:

There are 120 students who eat school lunch.

Of the total number of students, 1/2 of the students are in grades 3-5 that eat school lunch. How many 3-5 grade students eat school lunch?

Answer:

You know that 1/2 of the students are in grades 3-5, and the total number of students is 120, so you can use that information to find out how many students in grades 3-5 eat school lunch.

1/2 * 120 students = 60 students

So, 60 students in grades 3-5 eat school lunch.

*End of all QR codes & independent practice questions.

Proficiency Check 1

Hi Scholar! We are thrilled that you have worked so hard in this workbook! The following questions are used to show your knowledge of the math topics taught. We wish you the best as you continue to learn and grow!

Directions:
1. Answer each question to the best of your ability.
2. Use the additional space on the page to show your work.
3. Choose your answer by circling the letter or image.
4. Proceed to the next page.
5. Stop at **page 66**.

1. Multiply:

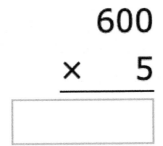

A. *3000*

B. 1100

C. 650

D. 560

2. What is the rule for this input/output table?

In	Out
1	2
4	8
5	10

A. Multiply 10

B. *Multiply 2*

C. Multiply 7

D. Multiply 6

3. This input/output table shows multiplication. What is the rule for this input/output table?

In	Out
0	0
1	6
2	12

A. Rule: Multiply 0

B. *Rule: Multiply 6*

C. Rule: Multiply 8

D. Rule: Multiply 5

4. Divide:

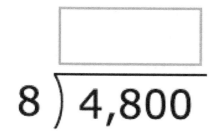

A. 200

B. 300

C. 800

D. *600*

5. What is the division rule for this input/output table?

In	Out
4	2
6	3
8	4

A. Divide 4

B. *Divide 2*

C. Divide 3

D. Divide 6

6. How is the rectangle divided?

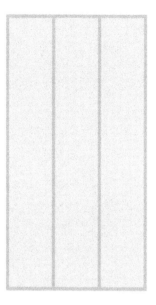

A. None of the above

B. Halves

C. *Thirds*

D. Fourths

7. Circle the letter or square that shows equal parts.

A.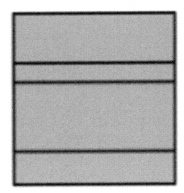

B.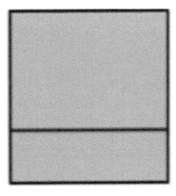

C. 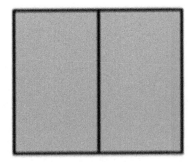   *C is the correct answer*

8. Circle the letter or shape that shows equal parts.

A.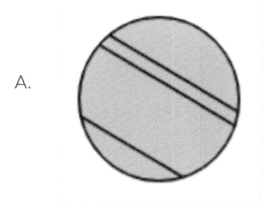

B. 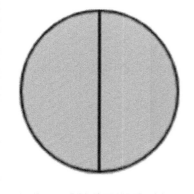   *B is the correct answer*

C.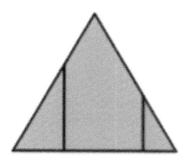

9. Which number line shows a bolded segment with a length of 1/2? Circle the number line.

The correct answer is #2

10. What fraction represents the shaded part?

A. 1/3

B. 1/4

C. *1/2*

D. 1/5

11. What is the value of the expression below?

$$5 + 2 \div 2$$

A. 7

B. 2

C. *6*

D. 3.5

12. What is the value of the expression below?

$$2 \times 2 + 4$$

A. 11

B. 12

C. *8*

D. 16

13. A treasure hunter discovered a buried treasure chest. She opened it up and discovered that it contained 973 diamonds and 2 rubies. How many gems were in the chest?

   A. 971

   B. *975*

   C. 1000

   D. 485

14. True's car broke down and she used $2 from her savings to have it repaired. After that, she had $690 left in savings. How much money did True have saved before her car broke?

  A. *692*

  B. 688

  C. 694

  D. 678

15. Mrs. Hall drove 4 miles to drop off her kids at school. Next, she drove 42 miles to work. At the end of the day, she drove 43 miles home. How many miles did she drive in all?

   A. 46

   B. 47

   C. 85

   D. *89*

Proficiency Check 2

Hi Scholar! We are thrilled that you have worked so hard in this workbook! The following questions are used to show your knowledge of the math topics taught. We wish you the best as you continue to learn and grow!

Directions:
1. Answer each question to the best of your ability.
2. Use the additional space on the page to show your work.
3. Choose your answer by circling the letter or image.
4. Proceed to the next page.
5. Stop at **page 81**.

1. Multiply

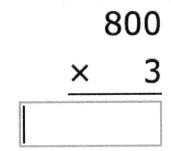

A. 1100

B. 300

C. *2400*

D. 500

2. If Old Navy can fit 5 sweaters in each shipping box, how many boxes should the company use to ship 20 sweaters?

   A. 1

   B. 4

   C. 5

   D. 3

3. What is the rule for this input/output table?

In	Out
0	0
1	3
2	6

A. *Multiply 3*

B. Multiply 2

C. Multiply 1

D. Multiply 6

4. What is the rule for this input/output table?

In	Out
4	2
8	4
10	5

A. Divide 4

B. Divide 3

C. *Divide 2*

D. Divide 1

5. Sharon went to the grocery store and bought 9 bagels. If there are 3 bagels in each pack, how many packs of bagels did Sharon buy?

　　A. *3*

　　B. 9

　　C. 6

　　D. 1

6. Which picture divides a rectangle in half?

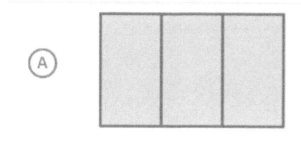

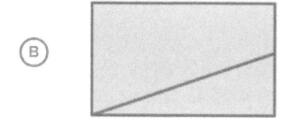

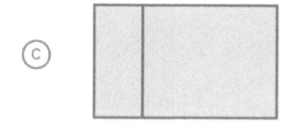

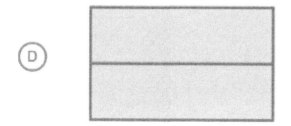

Answer: D

7. Which picture divides a rectangle into fourths?

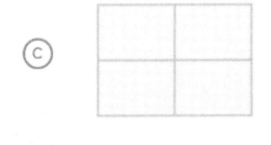

Answer: C

9. What fraction of the shape is shaded?

A. 1/2

B. 1/3

C. *1/8*

D. 1/4

10. What fraction of the shape is shaded?

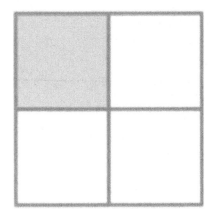

A. *1/4*

B. 1/2

C. 1/8

D. 1/6

11. What is the value of the expression below?

3 + 5 − 3

A. *5*

B. 6

C. 3

D. 2

12. What is the value of the expression below?

$5 + 1 \times 5$

A. 11

B. 30

C. *10*

D. 12

13. Kylie works at Chipotle. Over the weekend, she washed a combined total of 921 large and small plates. If Kylie washed 666 large plates, how many small plates did she wash over the weekend?

   A. 250

   B. *255*

   C. 666

   D. 921

14. Marvin owns a car dealership. Last week, he received a shipment of 220 cars. He now has 821 cars for sale. How many cars did Marvin have before the shipment?

   A. *601*

   B. 600

   C. 611

   D. 610

15. Angie is on the track team at school. Every weekday, 5 days a week, she runs 8 laps on the school track. For every 10 laps she finishes, Angie gets a little foot charm to put on a necklace. How many foot charms will Angie get this week?

    A. 3

    B. 4

    C. 5

    D. 6

*End of proficiency checks one and two.

ABOUT US

PRACTICE is a mission-driven business that believes in the power of public schools to build the next generation of urban-educated leaders. We are a New York City-based B-Corp that partners with principals, teachers and parents to close the opportunity gap in urban schools. Our work includes: a rigorous, culturally responsive curricula taught by Education Champions that look like the kids they serve, customized private tutoring solutions for one-on-one learning taught by our most accomplished Education Champions, and software solutions, built to help students succeed, that connect parents and educators and provide real-time insights and data from both inside and outside of the classroom.

VISION

No child's circumstance limits their potential.

MISSION

Advance equitable education for urban students to close the opportunity gap.

CORE VALUES

We have always been a mission driven organization and have had the same core values at PRACTICE since we started over a decade ago. We work incredibly hard to live our values at all levels of the company.

- Excellence - We expect nothing less from the students we serve

- Entrepreneurship – We recognize that innovation and execution are fundamental to improving educational outcomes

- Conscious Capitalism – We are focused on the triple bottom line: people (drivers of change), community (paying it forward), and profit (financial sustainability)

- Revolutionary Change - We seek to be the catalysts that positively disrupt the education status quo

BRAND PROMISES

We have always been a mission driven organization and have had the same core values at PRACTICE since we started over a decade ago. We work incredibly hard to live our values at all levels of the company.

- Programmatic Outcomes – We work relentlessly to meet the individual needs of our students to ensure progress is made towards achieving proficiency

- Professionalism – We hold ourselves to the highest standards from top to bottom

- Full Service Partnership – We do whatever it takes to deliver high quality products and services for our partners

FOUNDER + ORIGIN STORY

Founder and CEO Karim Abouelnaga started PRACTICE while in his dorm room at Cornell University. Karim was raised by a single mother on government aid in New York City where he attended some of the city's most struggling public schools. Thanks to a series of nonprofits and mentors, Karim became the first one in his family to attend college, graduating in the top 10% of his class.

In his first semester at Cornell, he realized the significant difference in his K-12 experience compared to that of many of his friends on campus. There, he rallied a group of classmates to create an organization to level the playing field for low-income children. Karim was determined to change the inequities he experienced in the public schools he grew up in to ensure that a student's zip code doesn't determine their future.

As CEO, Karim understands the importance of first-hand experience when working with urban schools and that is the foundation of our inside-out approach to education. Many of our leadership team and tutors are of and from the communities we serve. A majority of our tutors are college students working on undergraduate or graduate degrees who intimately understand the realities of urban classrooms and are driven to help urban students like themselves reach their full potential.

GRATITUDE

Thank you for supporting us! We started PRACTICE because we believed that all children – regardless of their race or socioeconomic status – have equal potential to compete intellectually in our society. Unfortunately, for poor, first-generation, Black and Latino youth, the supports necessary to enable them to reach their full potential are often forgotten. We are committed to rewriting that narrative. By partnering with PRACTICE, you are joining a community of champions who prioritize equity, access and the closing of the opportunity gap.

Have suggestions to strengthen our content? Visit our website www.practicebc.com and Contact Us with your feedback. We look forward to hearing from you!

Made in the USA
Middletown, DE
14 March 2023

26670549R00051